Emmeline Richardson

Sun, Moon And Stars

An Ownty Downty Book

Emmeline Richardson

Sun, Moon And Stars
An Ownty Downty Book

ISBN/EAN: 9783744753531

Printed in Europe, USA, Canada, Australia, Japan

Cover: Foto ©Thomas Meinert / pixelio.de

More available books at **www.hansebooks.com**

· SUN ·
· MOON · & · STARS ·
· AN ·
· OWNTY · DOWNTY ·
· BOOK ·

OF
PICTURES
AND · VERSES · FOR
CHILDREN · BY · E ·
RICHARDSON

JOHN · LANE · THE · BODLEY · HEAD ·
LONDON · & · NEW · YORK · 1899 ·

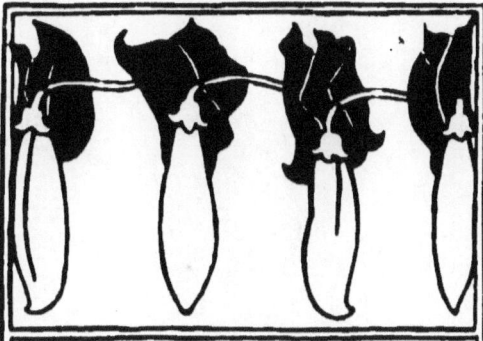

CONTENTS

	PAGE
Sun Moon and Stars	1
A Wish	4
Fairyland	5
The Spirit of the Woods	9
Rain Fairies	12
Lessons	15
In April	18
The Rainbow Land	21
Spring and Autumn	25

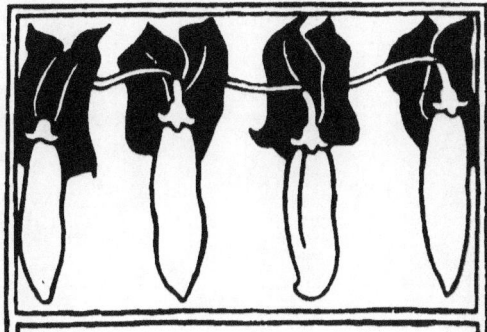

GOLD REGEN	29
THE BUTTERFLY	31
WINTER SONG	33
BLOW WINDS BLOW	35
THE CHANGELING	37
SUNSET GATES	40
BEDTIME	45
HORNS OF ELF-LAND	47
EVENSONG	49
THE STARS	50
MOONLIGHT SHINE	53
THE PINETREE	54
GOOD NIGHT	57

SUN·MOON·AND·STARS

The moon that smiles on
  you all night
The sun that laughs all
  day
The stars that twinkle
  twinkle go
Along the milky way

Sing loud to children
  day and night
Sing songs to all who
  hear
That all things are for
  their delight
And nothing is to fear.

Sing joyfully the whole
  year round
To children all that
  they
Should like the sun and
  moon be glad
And like the stars be
  gay.

CALIFORNIA

FAIRY LAND

Come down the fields
Come down with me
Come down to Fairyland,
Leave all your books &
work to see
And join the fairy band.

Across the meadow and
down the wood
A world of wonder lies
Where brownies bold
and fairies good
Look up with laughing eyes

From every leaf and
every flower
And every blade of grass
To welcome us in a
sunny hour
And to greet us as we pass

They frolic and dance in
the shady nooks
They skip and they run
in the sun
They peep from the brooks
with merry looks
And laughter & bubbling
fun.

Oh happy the days when
we reach that land!
Oh happy the hours when
we stay
And join in their revels
hand in hand
And share in their joyous
play!

Though the years will roll
over every soul
And we see the elves no
more
Yet the memory of those
joys we stole
Are ours forevermore.

THE SPIRIT OF THE WOODS

Deep in the heart of
the wood
Green green so green!
Where never a house
has stood
Never a man has been

There is the sprite of
the wood
Fair fair so fair!
Lovely her gracious mood
Lovely her shimmering
hair

Creep to that part of
the wood
Still still oh still!
Find her so tender and
good
Hear with an answering
thrill —

"Share the delight of the wood
Come come oh come!
Here is the fairest of food
Here is the happiest home

There is no strife in the wood
Wise wise be wise!"
No one has ever withstood
Her beckoning hands and eyes.

"Share the green life of the wood
Stay stay oh stay!"
She will carry you off like a flood
You never will wander away.

RAIN FAIRIES

Out of the sky they come
Down on the drops of rain
Down from the clouds above
Riding with might and main.

In shining coats of armour,
Their lances by their side,
—An army of rain fairies—
To war with dirt they ride.

They prance along the pavements
You can see their dan-cing feet
They wash the dingy houses
They wash the grimy street.

They dance through the
    dried-up country
They freshen the dusty
    fields
And they never rest till
    they finish their quest
And all dust to their
    onslaught yields.

They drive it all to
    the river
And away to the deep
    blue sea
And there it is lost
    forever
And they triumph
    gloriously.

Up in the sky the
    sun
Shines on the world
    again
Shines on the work
    well done
By the fairies of the
    rain.

THE ROOM IS HOT AND THE
   LESSONS ARE HARD,
AND HERE THEY SAY I
   MUST STAY
AND THE BLACKBIRD SINGS
 IN THE NEIGHBOURING YARD
"OH PLAY! OH PLAY! OH PLAY!"

THE SUN SHINES BRIGHT
  ON THE WORLD OUTSIDE
AND THE OTHERS HAVE
    GONE AWAY
AND THE WIND TO EVERY
   LEAF HAS CRIED
 BE GAY! BE GAY! BE GAY!"

CALIFORNIA

IN APRIL

"In April – month of smiles
and tears..
A little time you came
to stay
The sun laughed out as
if 'twere May
The fields put on their
best array
And the cuckoo cried to
listening ears
'In April – month of smiles
and tears.'"

And you – with spirit
brave and gay
Who smile through sorrow
and laugh down fears

With your tender face
And your wilful way
And your mood that
changes every day
And every change the
more endears
Like April — month of
smiles and tears.

Our hearts were sad and
the skies were grey
And the rain fell fast
When you went away
In April — month of
smiles and tears."

WHO NOW COULD
FRET OR MOPE?
TO THE WINDS OUR
CARES WE FLING
THE WINDS OF THE
LAND OF HOPE
THAT BLOW IN THE
TIME OF SPRING.

THE BLOSSOM WHI-
-TENED SLOPE
THE HILLS IN A
PURPLE RING
GIRD THE RAINBOW
LAND OF HOPE
THE RAINBOW LAND
OF SPRING.

THE PRIMROSE AND
HYACINTH OPE
AT THE FLASH OF THE
SWALLOW'S WING
AND COVER THE LAND
OF HOPE
AND BRIGHTEN THE
LAND OF SPRING.

Early in the morning
and the morning of
the year
when the light was
silver and the sky
was clear
I walked in the wood-
-lands and heard the
cuckoo's cry
and the twitter of
the little birds nest-
-ing near the sky.

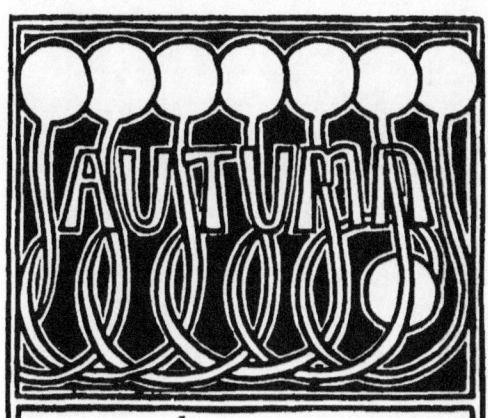

When the year was
waning and the end
was near
And the light was
fading golden in the
west
I walked in the wood-
-lands which the
rain left bleak and
drear
And saw above my
head the empty nest.

GOLD REGEN

IN WINTERTIME THE WATER
TURNED ICE AND SNOW-WHITE
RAIN
UPON THE TREES BARE BRANCHES
AS THICK AS LEAVES HAS
LAIN

AND WHEN THE COLD WAS
OVER
AND SPRING HAD COME
AGAIN
MIXT WITH THE FALLING
BLOSSOMS
THERE FELL A ROSY RAIN

BUT NOW BY THE LABUR-
-NAMS
BESIDE MY WINDOW PANE
GLOWING LIKE YELLOW
SUNSHINE
THERE IS ALWAYS GOLDEN
RAIN

THE BUTTERFLY

Ah, butterfly!
You that can leave the
earth
And reach the sky,
Whose wings have gained
their worth,
From rainbow dye,
Are happier far than I
Who cannot fly

All the bright day you
hie
From flower to flower
And all their sweetness
try
Or quiet lie
And sun yourself an
hour.

But summer days go by,
And then to die
Ah butterfly!

BLOW WINDS·BLOW

BLOW WINDS BLOW!
BLOW THE HEAVY CLOUDS
AWAY
THAT HAVE HID THE SUN
ALL DAY
DRY THE MEADOWS WHERE
WE PLAY
BLOW WINDS BLOW!

SHAKE THE RAINDROPS FROM
THE TREES
DRY THE FLOWERS AND
WAKE THE BEES
SING US ALL YOUR
HARMONIES
BLOW WINDS BLOW!

The Changeling

The magic wood is all
aflame tonight
Brighter and brighter
quivering gold and red
The old world fades before
this sunset light
Give me this world instead!

I hate their stifling towns
so cold and black
I am a stranger in this
world of men.
O come and take me
fairies, take me back
To fairyland again!

I cannot see you but I
hear you run
And rustle in the leaves,
O fairies dear!

I hear your happy voices
    call which none
but fairyfolk can hear.

I do remember faintly
    falteringly
Days long ago before I
    came to earth
In fairyland and now
    it seems to me
I am of fairy birth.

Surely you stole a mortal
    child and set
Me in his cradle in his
    place to grow
And thought that I would
    speedily forget
But I remember now.

The chill rains waste me
    & the harsh winds rack
And I am weary of the
    ache and pain
And lonely and forlorn,
    O take me back
To fairyland again!

SUNSET GATES

O CLOUDS THAT MOUNT ON HIGH
SAY WHAT YOU SEE THERE!
O CLOUDS THAT GILD THE SKY
WHAT MAY THERE BE THERE?
O CLOUDS THAT FLAME & FLY
FAIN WOULD WE FLEE THERE.

WHAT MAGIC PALACES
HIDE ALL THEIR SPLENDOUR
FAR IN THE BLUENESSES
STATELY AND TENDER,
RISE WHERE NO MALICE IS,
FEAR NO SURRENDER?

O BARS OF ROSE AND GOLD
SHOW WE BESEECH YOU
ALL THAT YOUR DEPTHS ENFOLD
ALL THAT THEY TEACH YOU
ALL THAT YOU HAVE & HOLD
FOR WE WOULD REACH YOU.

What radiant mysteries
Golden and green
Roseate fantasies
Still may be seen
Glimpses & gleams of these
Cloudrifts between!

Cloudlets oh tell us
Whither you wander
Active and zealous
Hither and yonder
You lure and compel us
Deeply to ponder.

Whence is your coming
Whither your going
Out of the gloaming
Into the glowing?
What in your roaming
Keep you from showing?
Where is your homing
From the wind's blowing?

Clouds of the sunset gates
Fair angel faces
Shine where your gold
    abates
Smile through your spaces
There Eldorado waits
There are our places.

BED-TIME

The great day's eye has
gone to rest
Behind the curtains of
the west.
The little day's-eyes
white and red
Are sleeping in the
garden bed.

Your little eyes of brown
and blue
Are growing tired and
sleepy too ·
And heavy hangs each
little head
Then come O children
come to bed :

Horns of Elfland

The sun has hidden be-
hind the hill
Which shone so blithe
since morn
The wind blows softly
through the trees
And hark! The fairies'
horn

The noises of the day
are still
The birds are hushed
to hear
To know another day
is sped
Another night is near

And now the elves put
forth their skill
And sweetest music
make
To call the sleepy stars
to shine
To call the moon to
wake.

THE STARS

Now that all the light
    has gone
And the pretty sunshine's
    done
From my window broad
    and high
I look up to see the
    sky.

There the stars come
    jumping out
Just like children with
    a shout
In a game of hide and
    seek
But the stars they never
    speak

Right across upon the hill
There are stars of earth
    as well
And by night these stars
    are seen
Where by day the streets
    have been.

VERY STRAIGHT AND IN A
ROW
UP ALONG AND DOWN THEY
GO
BUT THE BRIGHT LIGHTS
OF THE SKY
ALL GO MOST UNORDERLY.

WHEN I GO TO BED AT
NIGHT
ALL THESE STARS ARE
SHINING BRIGHT
BUT WHEN I GET UP
NEXT DAY
ALL THESE STARS HAVE
GONE AWAY

WHY DO THEY HIDE THEM-
SELVES BY DAY
I OFTEN WONDER WHY
- THE STARS THAT SPARKLE
ON THE HILL
AND SPARKLE IN THE
SKY ?

THE PINE TREE

Far out in the wood is
a great tall pine
Which overtops the
rest
Which blows in the wind
and grows in the shine
And looks to the east
and west
To the north and south
in rain and fine
And guards the ring-
dove's nest

When the night is
stormy and gustily
The noisy winds do
blow
That tree talks all
night just to me
And what it says I
know
And it drops its fir-
cones lustily
For me on the ground
below.

Some time when the wind
blows through the trees
and the stars and moon
are bright
I'll ride through the air
upon the breeze
and up to the pine-tree's
height
And look abroad far
as it sees
And talk to the moon
all night.

I'll ask the moon about
everything
And the stars with their
blinking eyes,
For they've watched the
world since the earliest
spring
And they are old and
wise
And I know they will
answer my questioning
And will give me true
replies.

GOOD·NIGHT

GOOD NIGHT· GOOD NIGHT·
THE LITTLE STARS ARE
SHINING
LAY DOWN YOUR HEAD
AND SLEEP
LEAVE ALL YOUR MAKE-
BELIEVE WITHOUT RE-
·PINING
YOUR GAMES AND TOYS
WILL KEEP·

GOOD NIGHT· GOOD NIGHT·
FORGET TODAY'S BRIEF
SORROW
TODAY'S GLAD LAUGHTER
AND TODAY'S DELIGHT
SLEEP TILL THE SUN SHALL
WAKE YOU TO TOMORROW
FROM HAPPY DREAMS
TONIGHT

www.ingramcontent.com/pod-product-compliance
Lightning Source LLC
Chambersburg PA
CBHW020119170426
43199CB00009B/568